Joel Foote Bingham

National Disappointment

A Discourse, Occasioned by the Delivered in Westminster Church, Buffalo

Joel Foote Bingham

National Disappointment
A Discourse, Occasioned by the Delivered in Westminster Church, Buffalo

ISBN/EAN: 9783744754019

Printed in Europe, USA, Canada, Australia, Japan

Cover: Foto ©Suzi / pixelio.de

More available books at **www.hansebooks.com**

National Disappointment.

A

DISCOURSE

OCCASIONED BY THE

ASSASSINATION OF PRESIDENT LINCOLN

DELIVERED IN WESTMINSTER CHURCH, BUFFALO.

SUNDAY EVENING, MAY 7TH, 1865

BY JOEL F. BINGHAM,

PASTOR OF THE CONGREGATION.

BUFFALO:
BREED, BUTLER AND COMPANY.

1865.

DISCOURSE.

I WILL BRING THE BLIND BY A WAY THAT THEY KNEW NOT.—ISAIAH
XLII, 16.

No other fact has been more conspicuous
upon the face of society among us, during the
progress of the war that is now closing, than
the constantly spreading and deepening sentiment of our national dependence on the allot-
ments of the Divine Hand. We have learned,
with all our fellow-countrymen, during the
last four years, as we never before understood
it, the uncertainty of human calculations, and
the double blindness of human self-sufficiency,
conceit and independence. Inexorable and
repeated disappointments have taught us — the
most careful estimates and the most sanguine
expectations, now immeasurable cut short, and
then immeasurably outrun, have taught us,

thoroughly at last, that God, above all earthly forces, still directs the destinies of this world, and, by an inscrutable and irresistible Providence, WILL BRING BLIND MEN INTO HIS PURPOSES, (*nationally as well as individually*,) BY A WAY THEY KNEW NOT.

At the outset of the rebellion, we were both unwilling and unable to believe that a civil war among us would ever actually come, till the sudden bombardment and fall of Sumter thrilled, like lightning, through the national heart, in the terrible conviction that civil war was already begun. So, the blind eyes of the people were then opened, so far as to see that the incredible crisis was upon us, and their heart was so far fired, as to rouse them to gird themselves for the dreadful strife. But the magnitude of the treason which was on foot, and the time and force which would be required to crush it was not then perceived, and only dawned on our dull vision in the mortifying and overwhelming defeat of the national arms at Bull Run. Thus, again, we were strained to the sending of those huge armies into the field which have swept with desolation from

the Potomac to the Gulf, and have destroyed
at once the status of Rebellion and the status
of Slavery. Slavery, however, even then, we
meant not to disturb, and commander after
commander was removed in disgrace for smiting it, even as a military blow upon the
strength of the public enemy. But the
tedious and unsuccessful campaigns in Virginia,
the dreadful disasters on the Peninsula, before
Fredericksburg, in the Valley of the Shenan-
doah, and especially the alarming irruptions of
the rebel armies into Pennsylvania and Mary-
land, threatening the destruction of Washington, and even of our great northern cities —
it was this terrible path of God which
brought us, in the peril of our existence, to
lift our hand with the might of despair, and
sweep utterly from our soil that accursed
system of wrong under which rebellion was
born, and by which it was mightily fostered,
even in its grapple upon the throat of our
liberties. By such bitter disappointments and
terrors, were the President and the nation
nerved up to utter, (with doubt and hesita-
tion,) the immortal proclamation of January 1,
1863, by which the heathenish shackles were

knocked at a blow from four millions of
wretched fellow-beings, at whose outrageous
wrongs humanity had wept for ages, though
powerless to break the tremendous strength,
or alleviate the horrors of their iron bondage.
See then, fellow citizens, in these bitter sur-
prises, how gloriously God has led us, in our
blindness, by a way of His own that we
knew not.

But these things are now securely past.
We have been coming, in these preparatory
remarks, to speak of our recent tremendous
surprise and grief. For surely we expected
no such thing. We have been equally con-
founded with amazement, and crushed with
sorrow. We did not dream that the path
along which God was leading us, already
actually emerging, as it seemed, forever, from
the darkness and peril under which we had
wept for four long years — we did not dream
that this path, of Providence, already so
cheering, and brightening every day with the
realization of our best hopes, was to turn
again into the gloom of that bitter sorrow
which overspreads the land. That the great
and good man whom we all delighted to

honor — that the twice chosen President of the now regenerated nation — the President, beyond all question, who was beloved with a tenderer affection, and a more nearly unanimous sentiment among the people, than any other who has occupied that seat of power and of popular criticism, save, perhaps, the first, the unopposed, the uncompared, the solitary Washington, who is now henceforth to divide his glory with this second object of a nation's eternal veneration — a man, too, not only of rare and tried wisdom, of an integrity as high as heaven above every bribe, and of a patriotism burning like the flame of life itself, but a man so gentle, so conciliatory and forgiving, so unwilling to inflict pain even upon the guilty — a man of such transparent honesty, of such child-like simplicity — the very embodiment of every kind and sweet and almost womanly virtue of our nature — that this man, the embodiment, also, of the supreme authority of the nation, God's anointed over us — truly, but a few days ago, nothing short of an accredited prophecy from the skies could have made us believe that this incomparable President, this intensely beloved man,

this representative of our national power and
our national life — that he would fall a mur-
dered victim to the bloody work of a political assasin. When the terrible news first
sounded in our ears we could not believe the
tidings. We can now scarcely credit the tes-
timony of our senses. But for three live-long
weeks we have been dwelling in the midst of
weeds. Every home in the land has been
draped in mourning. The temples of public
authority, law and justice, and the sanctuaries
of religion of every name, from Maine to
Louisiana, stand robed in black. We have all
witnessed and mingled in the funeral *cortege*,
magnificent in signs of woe. Many of us have
gazed with our eyes upon the blackened ruin,
fast crumbling back into unrecognizable dust
— all of the nation's Deliverer and Slavery's
Destroyer which the murderer's work has left
to a mourning people.

Now we have to ask *what that new light
is which God has just made to dawn on our
slow vision by this new and terrible turn in
the path of His Providence.* The occasion of
such mighty mourning — a nation bowed, and
each man for himself bowed in the agony of

a personal bereavement — what has this reveal-
ed to us which, in our blindness, we were before overlooking? What now are the new, or
at least newly reiterated and re-emphasized
facts which these blackened heavens are thun-
dering in the ears of the nation?

Why, in the first place, what all good men
have been slow to read, and unwilling to
read, but are now compelled to read in letters of blood and fire in the heavens — *that
the animus of this rebellion — the spirit which
gave it life, and which has been its living
principle ever since* — IS ABSOLUTELY
HELLISH TO THE LAST DEGREE. For it
were useless to attempt to shield the cause of
rebellion, from responsibility for, and compli-
city with, this last supreme culmination of
its guilt and murder. It were useless to talk
of this deed, which has shocked and disgusted
the world, as merely the individual guilt of a
maddened villain. Supposing, for a · moment,
that, in point of fact, it had been so, (which
is now officially proven to have been far otherwise,) yet then, even, what must have been
the seed, the atmosphere, the culture which
could germinate and ripen this accursed fruit!

2

No good cause, no laudable spirit, no worthy end could inspire a man to such devilish deeds. The cause, its spirit, its end are unmistakably set forth, before heaven and earth, in the fiendish champion and his fiendish work.

But the almost incredible truth has been made as clear as noonday — the unwelcome evidence has rolled up in masses of terrible light over innumerable enterprises and deeds of darkness, till one must be more sightless than the blind who does not see, to-day, that the nameless act of April 14th was but striking a higher and more conspicuous note in the same dreadful harmony of hell, which has been playing, half-muffled and in the distance, for the last four years, the name of which is "Revenge and Ruin." The accomplishment of this very deed was but narrowly escaped, at Baltimore, four years ago. That attempt was, indisputably, in the hands of the leaders of revolt. It was intended to forestall the inevitable struggle, and render an appeal to arms impossible. Six months ago, when re-election was certain, it was coolly advertised for, in the newspapers, at a magnificent reward.

Commencing at Selma, Georgia, (a copy of which I have seen,) the offer was copied from paper to paper, till it had spread throughout the South; and at least one prominent Southern journal, mentioning the project with applause, took occasion to urge upon the attention of the leaders, at Richmond, that a few millions appropriated in this way would be certain to secure the fact, and would achieve more for the cause, than hundreds of millions spent in the regular prosecution of civilized warfare. This course, however attractive, the leaders dare not *openly* take. It was too perilous, thus to outrage the conscience of all civilized mankind. Yet it has now transpired that they were *privy* to a most formidable conspiracy, to prevent, in this same diabolical way, the second inauguration on the 4th of March last, which, no thanks to them, miscarried.

Look, now, for a moment, at the Southern methods of prosecuting their public and civilized warfare, so-called, which the late climax of crime has powerfully illuminated. In Virginia, arsenic was thrown into the wells, where national armies were likely to pass; and the inhabitants of the country, whom these

armies had spared in life and property, were
employed to bring into the national camps
and sell to these soldiers poisoned pies and
fruit. Sheridan himself, early in the summer
of 1864, barely escaped with his life from a
fatal dose received in a similar way.

Throughout the territory in rebellion, and
during the whole contest, numberless murderous gangs have swept to and fro, hunting
out and chasing down, like wild beasts, every
man, however unarmed, unoffending and quiet,
against whom the faintest suspicion whispered
that he still loved, and, in the bottom of his
heart, still clung to, the flag and the government of his fathers. Once caught, these
"faithful among the faithless found," whose
only offence was loyalty, were treated with
every refinement of cruelty and murder. They
were butchered in the midst of their families.
They were hung upon trees in front of their
own door. They were starved to death in the
forests. They were waylaid and shot from the
wayside. Their houses were set on fire over
their heads, and their wives and infant children driven naked into the night and the
storm and the wilderness.

Our children will be compelled to read with
a shudder of the wholesale massacres of hundreds and thousands of national troops after
surrender; of wounded national soldiers, on the
field of battle and in the power of the enemy,
purposely left to welter and languish, for days,
without attendance, or so much as the service
of a drop of water for their terrible thirst; of
unnecessary and cruel amputations, by rebel
surgeons, with the double purpose, openly
avowed, to punish and disable; of hospitals
purposely set on fire, with sick and wounded
national soldiers left, by scores, to roast and
consume in the burning building; in short, of
the fortunes of battle, so terrible at the best,
savagely aggravated, in a thousand horrible
ways, by the inhuman and unheard of barbarities which this rebellion has developed.

Our children and the world will read, too,
with indescribable detestation, how great and
peaceful cities, far remote from the armies in
conflict, were secretly set on fire, by the skulking
incendiaries of the rebellion; of the attempted
destruction of moving railroad trains, filled with
unarmed men, women and children, by similar
emissaries from the same quarter; and of the

cruelest ocean piracies on record, perpetrated in ships of foreign make and outfit, under this monstrous assumption of illegitimate authority.

But the blackest page, as it seems to me, which the whole history of the past can show will be that on which shall stand the yet unwritten, yet ungathered and unknown summary of *the horrors of the rebel prisons*, which confined and slowly destroyed the soldiers captured from the national armies — pits of torture, where a deliberate, systematic, long protracted process of freezing, infection and starvation was coolly and unrelentingly carried forward upon tens of thousands of men taken in open battle, and carried forward in connection with circumstances of brutality whose horror is beyond expression, and which the ear of decency refuses to hear. Our posterity will turn pale as they read that record. Mankind will execrate the story with everlasting curses, and confess that this alone were enough to consign the exploded slave-holders' rebellion to the blackest abyss of human infamy.

Now it should seem strange, if it were not found, (though the evidence which has transpired all points in the opposite direction,) nevertheless, it were strange, that some of the cooler heads among the insurgent authorities should not have foreseen the reactionary effect which a knowledge of these barbarities must of necessity work to the prejudice of their cause, and, however careless as to the atrocities in themselves, should not have felt compelled to put a stop to this disgraceful and self-damaging course. But the important fact is that these atrocities have not been stopped, in any direction, from the beginning until now. On the contrary, history will be compelled to declare, that this rebellion, from the first, has clothed itself with every possible atrocity as with a garment. There is nothing whatever that its partisans have scrupled to do. Unexampled perjuries, deceit and theft, the most dreadful and extensive persecution of neighbors and fellow citizens, piracies of the most outrageous character, wholesale poisoning, mining of prisoners' quarters, ready for the match, in case they were likely to be retaken, massacres, tortures, starvation of tens of thousands of prisoners of war, the destruction of railway trains, the conflagration of great cities full of peaceful inhabitants by the nightly torch of the incendiary, and finally, oh heavens! the concerted butchery of the President of the United States, by a too long tolerated play-actor!

The evidence which is daily transpiring points, as we have said, with increasing certainty to the conclusion, (hard as it is to credit both the stupidity of the mistake and the brutality of the guilt,) that the head and representative and for a time essentially the dictator over the whole insurrectionary movement — the eternally infamous Davis — that he and his coadjutors could, in a great degree, at least, have checked and prevented this career of inhuman proceedings, but did not; because their better judgment was clouded by crime, and even their desire for the surest success, overpowered by a terrible thirst for revenge — a result which might naturally enough be expected from that spirit of hate and destruction to which they surrendered their souls, when they entered the conspiracy to break up and destroy this gentlest of governments and happiest of nations on earth. This view, it must be confessed,

is corroborated, also, by the reflection that
the incredible starvation horrors at the Libby
Prison in Richmond, especially, to say nothing of the corresponding horrors at Belle
Isle, at Salisbury, N. C., at Danville, Va., at
Andersonville and elsewhere, must have been
dependent on the will of the President, as
commander-in-chief of the rebel forces. He
must have known perfectly the facts.
Whether the cruelties were first begun by
his order, or not, he could, it seems certain, have spoken a word, or given a stroke
of his pen, which would have sent relief
and life to these dying men. But this he
did not do. That word he did not speak.
Their cruel and unnecessary deaths, therefore,
it is scarcely possible to deny, cry out of
the ground by thousands, and call him their
relentless murderer.

But there is another possible explanation of
the strength and steadiness of that unbroken
current of brutalities and fiendish deeds. We
are able to suppose, that, the rebellion once
under way, the leaders were practically unable altogether to control its lawless spirit, and
restrain its hideous excesses. It is not im-

probable, perhaps — though we must confess
that there is not a morsel of evidence to sustain the supposition — yet it is conceivable, at
least, that the rebelling leaders, from motives
of far-sighted policy, however malignant their
passions might be, never advised to these cruelties and brutalities, but counseled to the
opposite course, and resisted, even, the actual
perpetration. We say it is conceivable that it
may have been so; and if this be the true
alternative; if the spirit of rebellion has developed a fury and madness which its leaders
could not restrain ; if it has seized the bits in
its teeth, and run unmanageable into outrageous inhumanities from which its instigators
may well endeavor to extricate themselves
with repudiation and shame and alarm; if it
be *so*; if this, rather than the other, be the
true explanation of these atrocities ; yet in
what respect is the situation alleviated, whether
as to the more than murderous guilt of the
instigating leaders, or as to the terrible character of the now developed and maddened
spirit of misrule and destruction? Oh, how
irreparable and eternal, is the mischief, and
how unpardonable is the thousandfold murder-

ous guilt of those desperate men who have persistently roused, and lashed into an ungovernable fury, this demoniac temper which in the fruitless support of an abominable cause has deluged a happy continent with human blood, and gloated over thousands of the most blissful homes on earth covered with blight, desolation and woe! Oh, there are crimes *so big* and *so dreadful*, as almost to paralyze our sense of right and wrong, and we stand in a kind of uncertainty and bewilderment before their tremendous guilt! Fellow citizens, it is madness to talk of pardon and amnesty for such men. In a civil sense they have committed the unpardonable sin, for which there can be no forgiveness. The history of the world has invariably shown that a weak pity for the guilty is cruelty to the innocent. The only possible stability for our Government, and safety for our children, depends on the irrevocable doom of these men, who stand before heaven and earth the murderers at once of ourselves and our liberties.

But this disposal of the leaders in treason, painful and difficult as it may be, is not the most painful, nor the most difficult aspect of our situation. It is comparatively easy, (though I confess to much misgiving, lest the government and the nation shall prove morbidly and dangerously merciful in this quarter, even,) yet it is comparatively easy to deal with a few conspicuous traitors; but we shall be terribly deceived if we imagine that this will either remove or paralyze the dreadful and now maddened spirit of rebellion, revenge, and ruin. We hear dangerous syrens in one quarter and another singing delusive strains of pity and pardon. "The spirit of vengeance" against us, we hear it said in some high conservative quarters, "the spirit of vengeance is now quelled. The war is over. The day has gone by for anger, severity and alarm." No assertion could be more untrue. None could be more perilous for us to accept in such a time as this. We do not speak of the almost indifferent masses. They did not excite the war. But there are hearts, by hundreds, and I know not but by thousands, in which the spirit of vengeance is not quelled, and never will be, while they breathe in earthly air. Consider, we pray you, how astonishingly, beyond all we were able to believe possible, the spirit of treason and blood grew

strong and spread, by the fostering care of
its early fomenters, even under the peaceful
skies of our former visible unity and fraternity.
How rank and widely extended, then, must
have become its growth, under the congenial
tempests and malignity of these four years of
visible separation and exasperating war? Its
purposes are now defeated, but its disposition
is unchanged, except as it is now the more
frenzied by chagrin and despair. It is but a
specimen of this sublimated venom which, be
it remembered, since the hopeless collapse of
their cause, and when the door of peace was
already opening, has filled our land with
blacker mourning, than the united slaughters
of the whole war. From this horrible specimen Providence is calling us to learn of the
spirit which is yet to be dealt with.

How long this state of things is to continue
— how long this temper of murderous treason
is to remain, suppressed, indeed, but not dead
— how long it is to exist, scattered and con-
cealed, but alive and rankling in embittered
and desperate bosoms, or perhaps fostered and
deliberative in the darkness of secret organi-
zations — this is the first and foremost of the

great questions on which our national destiny is now hinged; and the tremendous interests which it involves are equalled only by the tremendous uncertainty that hangs over it, and utterly baffles every attempt to predict, or calculate its future developments. To await these developments would be to await perdition. The contingency to be instantly met, with all its uncertainties, is already upon us. Its uncertainties constitute a great part of its peril, as well as its demand for immediate, effectual and decisive remedies.

In times like these it must be wise, then, for us and our rulers to recall, and to be willing to take for the guidance of our conduct, principles of safety which have been so often demonstrated, at the cost of seas of human blood on other continents and in former generations. We cannot afford, in days like these, to throw history and experience aside, in order to make trial of humanitarian theories and crude speculations. The exigency calls for well-aimed and rapid strokes, such as the experience of the world has proved to be efficacious and sure.

Among the principles which have been

settled by the bloody experiments of all the
ages, and stand written in blood-red letters
along all the pages of the past, one of the
first is, that treason, the *crimen majestatis*, is
not only in its own character the supremest
pitch of human guilt, but also always contains,
potentially, in its black bosom, all possible
crimes; and, by the common consent of the
civilized world, whoever enters into a treason-
able conspiracy, openly takes his life in his
hand, and voluntarily sets up in the sight of
all mankind, as the stake of his success in
quenching the life of his government, his own
death, poverty and infamy. Another of the
principles which belong to this same category
is, that the stability of human government
indispensably requires a conviction pervading
the minds of all its subjects, of the certainty
that law will be executed, penal justice in-
flicted, legal equity maintained, in spite of
opposition and combinations, no matter how
formidable, and at the cost, even, if necessary,
of the happiness,·the reputation, the property,
the life of individuals, no matter how nu-
merous, no matter of what station. It is also
one of the stern facts which have been estab-

lished by experience, that the spirit of murder cannot be cured by caresses. It has most commonly been the gentlest of governments, and the most generous of rulers, that have fallen by treason and murder. Republics, in comparison with monarchies, have ever been notoriously insecure, and, for the most part, have been finally destroyed by traitors from within. So, as a rule, has it been of gentle, unsuspicious, large-hearted rulers in dangerous times. It was not Herod, dripping with the blood of the innocents, but Julius Cæsar, the most generous of men, who fell at the foot of Pompey's statue, by the daggers of *pardoned* conspirators. It was not the infamous Catharine de Medicis, of France, the patroness of profligates and assassins, the instigator of the massacre of St. Bartholomew, but it was the lovely, peerless Henry IV., the mildest, wisest, most paternal prince France ever saw, who fell by Ravaillac's knife, in the streets of Paris, and covered France with unexampled mourning. It was not Philip II. of Spain, the meanest, cruelest, darkest spirit that ever occupied a throne, but it was William of Orange, the brave, devoted, glorious deliverer of Holland, the idol of his people, who was shot, at the door of his dining-room at Delft, by a hired assassin of Philip. It was not the arch-traitor Davis, hated and cursed as he was by his out-lawed coadjutors, and yet likely to get away with his life, but it was the gentle, forbearing, forgiving, the incomparably loved and honored President Lincoln, who received the assassin's ball, and whose untimely and cruel death has filled every loyal heart in the land with unut-terable sorrow.

These principles, which ought to be worth to us, whatever our lives and fortunes and liberties are worth, are familiar and easily apprehended; and the inferences which of necessity follow are certain and terrible. These principles, we say, and the stern and terrible inferences which they carry, have just been written, anew, over the heads of this nation, as it were, in letters of fire and blood on a midnight sky. Nevertheless we have not recalled these things with a view to dictate, nor with the desire that you, or that our fellow citizens at large, should dictate in their hearts, even, much less should clamor-ously prescribe to our rulers and tribunals

4

what kind, or what measure, of punishment
shall be meted out to the various partici-
pants and abettors of this fearful but now
smitten and dying rebellion — who shall die,
who shall be exiled, who disfranchised and
left at home, who, from various reasons of
public expediency, pardoned and restored.
No good, as it appears to us, is to be hoped
for, but great damage is to be apprehended,
from such discussion. In the case of an
ordinary, everyday crime, it is by common
consent admitted to be unwise and improper
to discuss the measure of punishment, before
the constituted authorities have sifted both
facts and expediences, and passed the lawful
decision. Much more must it be so in a case
like the present, of such transcendent magnitude, and of such an unexampled character.
Opinions will be sure to differ in respect to
details; partisanship is easiest kindled and
passions blaze most furiously over such personal material, and dissension cannot fail to re-
tard and render more uncertain that stroke of
justice which all desire to see fall, in some
form, upon the guilty; while, too, the most
essential thing, and perhaps the only thing

really vital to the republic is, that the stroke of retribution should be at once sure and speedy.

But, unquestionably, as the whole class of facts to which we have just alluded, and above all the terrible fact which has brought us to this discussion to-night, distinctly indicate, *the danger which chiefly threatens us lies not in the direction of severity, but in that of leniency* — we are in no danger whatever of being too severe, but we are in great danger of an easy indifference. Severity was never a popular virtue, because its face looks unlovely, at first sight, and, especially, to a crowd, and also because its exercise requires of most men an effort and a self-sacrifice which the majorities, unless stimulated by some great excitement. like that with which God is now stimulating us, are seldom or never ready to undertake. Unquestionably, a few weeks ago, when the last great support of the rebellion gave way to our arms, and the speedy end .of all armed resistance to the government flashed upon our view, then, our very success was operating to overset our safety. The joy of final victory, the inexpressible sense of relief

in every mind, and the exuberance of our
rose-colored hopes, unfortunately, but not un-
naturally, went at once to melt down the
sternness of the popular heart, and efface the
just sense of wrong and danger which were
still indispensable to key the national nerve
up to the thorough work of annihilating the
last fragment of treason.

But if, after the new and terrible light
which this fearful Providence has thrown upon
the spirit and purposes of treason among us —
if, after this wholesome alarm, which has
touched the minds of millions who would not
otherwise have seen, or believed, the great
and insiduous perils by which we are still en-
compassed — if, after all, we now fail to put
the stern and necessary and finishing hand to
the tottering and skulking remnants of this
rebellion, smiting with every most effective
blow, till the last fibre of its existence is an-
nihilated, beyond resuscitation and beyond
resurrection — then what will be the judgment
of history upon us, and who will pity our
miseries, or, should we be utterly devoured by
endless treason, who would drop a tear on

the page that should record our national ex-
tinction?

But, thanks to the kind efficiency of
God's bitter strokes, this will not be. Our
last lesson has been enough. The American
people is ready, now, to sustain, with unflinch-
ing determination, the execution of law and
justice and expediency, both upon the shat-
tered carcass, and upon every existing limb,
of this hideous treason; and no matter how
terrible and how extensive the application of
punishment may be, they are ready to make
the welkin ring with their contented and
hearty Amen!

The American Government has passed, and
emerged in safety, from the crucial test of its
lawful authority and its power to maintain it.
It is settled, whether the United States be a
nation, living an indivisible unity of life, or
whether it be a loose and lifeless conglomer-
ation of thirty-six supreme sovereignties. That
troublesome folly is no longer debatable,
whether the will of a State, or of any co-
alition of States, can effectually defy the authority of the American people, as embodied
in the General Government. These heresies

have found their end. They have been ground
to powder in the shocks of battle, and tram-
pled into the dust of the Southern planta-
tions under the terrible marches of the national armies.

Above all, that cause of causes — that force
behind all other forces — that germinating
power and foster-father of the States' rights
heresy — that heaven-assaulting system of sin
— legalized slavery — has been throttled in the
exigencies of war, and its very carcass, in
the smoke of battle, has disappeared. This
was a way of deliverance, and advancement,
which we knew not, and four years ago were
too blind to see, but by which God (glory
to His name) has astonishingly brought us.

The immediate instrument by whom we
have been thus led — blindly indeed and
through terrible alarms, yet safely and gloriously led — has been, I need not say, the
departed, lamented, venerated President, whose
precious dust, the nation, sobbing in the
agony of bereavement, have just followed with
benedictions to the place which shall give it
an honored rest, till the morning of the
resurrection. He has not only deserved to

be, but he has been, the most fortunate of men. Well might the most illustrious of emperors envy his fame. His history is sublime. His glory is peerless.

There is but one measure of greatness and glory which the American people will ever tolerate to be used, in attempting to estimate the grandeur of his excellence, and the brightness of his name. Upon a monumental column, at the northeast corner of Trafalgar Square, in London, stands, in marble, the immortal Nelson, evermore attracting the gaze of the multitudes which are surging along at his feet, and reminding them of patriotism, valor and glory. The opposite, northwest corner has a similar pedestal column, but its empty top has been for fifty years awaiting the coming hero who should be found worthy to stand in marble beside the glorious Admiral, and divide with him the silent instruction of the surging, admiring throng. Mount Vernon, in the south of our land, planted on the bosom of slavery and chivalry, has hitherto held the form of the one great glory of our nation, whither pilgrims trod to admire the character of Washington, and receive new inspirations of liberty and patriotism, at his tomb. The prairie of the north, in an atmosphere of purer freedom and sterner toil, has been standing, an empty pedestal, in the sight of heaven, though we knew it not, awaiting through these sixty-five years, the tomb of the coming hero who should be worthy to divide with the Father of his country the applause and the inspiration of posterity. The path of patriot pilgrims will henceforth branch alike northward and southward to the resting place equally of the Founder of American Liberty, and of the Destroyer of American Treason and Traitorous Slavery. The two niches of glory are now full. Let us accustom our eyes to the glittering letters of immortality, and our ears to the golden sound which our children's children will chant, together, to the latest generation — WASHINGTON and LINCOLN! WASHINGTON and LINCOLN!!

The few great names grow greater and more glorious, as years go by. They require the perspective of ages, to allow us to make a true measurement of their vastness; and it is only the calm atmosphere of written history, and the increasing light of developing truth, which is able to bring out, and will continue more and more to bring out, in the apprehension of mankind, their real splendor. So it has been with WASHINGTON, the first of our golden names, so it will be with LINCOLN, our second.

There are reasons which will render this law of human glory more sure in the second case, than it has been in the first. WASHINGTON was a *military chief* — a position which always affords the best opportunity for building up a rapid fame of the most showy and captivating kind. He was gilded, at once, with the whole military glory of his country's successful arms. The just departed LINCOLN, though officially and truly commander-in-chief of the armies and navies of the nation, controlling with marvelous firmness, sagacity and singleness of purpose, the whole complicated machinery of this tremendous war, and having finally organized and achieved for the nation a general and conclusive victory, (so far as any human chief can, reverently, be said to have organized a victory, in affairs so immense and complicated beyond any sure calculations of man,) yet wore no other uniform but the dress of an

American citizen, he rode at the head of no
armies, he remained in the shade of his offi-
cial closet, he was absorbed in thought and
prayer, he was toiling in silence at the heavy
cares of civil policy, and he was listening
to the plea of the distressed. The immediate applause of successful arms he gladly
left for his faithful and illustrious lieutenants
in the field, who richly deserve their fame;
while, nevertheless, many a specific and un-
expected blow which fell with crushing weight
upon the bleeding head of the rebellion was
contrived and matured in his own original and
sagacious brain.

Then again, WASHINGTON was not called
to encounter a breath of *political prejudice*, in
his opening career, but rode at once to his
illustrious station, on a whirlwind of popular
choice, esteem and expectation. The just departed LINCOLN fell upon far different times,
and encountered a far different beginning. He
was sharply opposed. He was extensively and
outrageously defamed. Even by his friends, he
was then but partially known, and relied on
with many painful misgivings and fears, which
gave way but slowly at first, though they disap-

peared more and more rapidly, as the splendor of his integrity and the richness of his affections and the clearness of his insight and the invincibility of his purpose and his flaming patriotism, began to form that wonderful halo of glory which shone so brightly, at last, around his venerated head.

Another thing — which fixes a stronger impression upon contemporaries than on posterity, and the essential splendor of which steadily vanishes as ages go by — *the family* of WASHINGTON was old, dignified and wealthy; and these factitious advantages, never to be despised in gilding a contemporary renown, possessed, unquestionably, a greater influence upon the men of his times, than they would exert among us to-day. The just departed LINCOLN has gathered no temporary dignity from this quarter, and while, therefore, the brightness of his name will never fade in the least by the depreciation of such honor, on the contrary, even the romantic enchantment that gathers about the name of Cincinnatus, taken from the plough-field to the command and the salvation of the Roman state, will weave its peculiar and increasing witchery of glory, around the strange, homely origin of "the people's President."

Finally, WASHINGTON *lived* for his country, and died as a great and good man would wish to die, who had no more sacrifices to make for his fellow men. The life of the just departed LINCOLN, after having wrought out the painful salvation of the Republic, has been offered, a bloody sacrifice, upon the altar of human freedom and the happiness of his fellow countrymen. He has taken the last degree of glory, and set above his undying name the martyr's crown. The best who shall arise among us, in the future, may imitate, but none can surpass him. Further than his, human effort and human glory cannot go.

"Shroud the banner! rear the cross!
Consecrate a nation's loss!
Lay the gentle son of Toil!
Proudly in his native soil;
Crowned with honor to his rest,
Bear the Prophet of the West!"

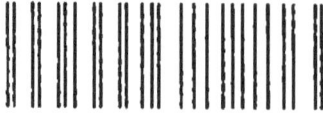

www.ingramcontent.com/pod-product-compliance
Lightning Source LLC
Chambersburg PA
CBHW021433090426
42739CB00009B/1466